THIS JOURNAL BELONGS TO:

Published by The Regenerative Writing Institute

Copyright © 2019 by Gina Tang
All rights inherent.
Please ask for permission to reproduce, scan, or distribute in any printed or electric form.

ISBN 978-1-950779-00-0

This publication is designed to provide creative encouragement in regard to the subject matter covered. The author does not claim to offer medical, legal, financial, or other professional services.

TO BECOMING
THE MOTHER
OF YOUR DREAMS.

MOTHERHOOD IS VALUABLE AND DAMN-BLOODY-HARD, LIKE A DIAMOND. THERE ARE RICH MOMENTS, OF COURSE. AND I LOVE MY CHILDREN. BUT THE HOURS SPENT—BRUTE SWEAT INVESTMENT—FEEDING AND FIXING AND CLEANING AND CALMING AND EVERY OTHER TASK—SHORT AND TALL, BIG AND SMALL—START TO FEEL LIKE ALL THESE TENTACLES WRAPPED AROUND MY BODY-MIND, UNTIL I FIND MYSELF RACING TO SOME SORT OF FINISH LINE, IF ONLY I CAN KEEP MY FOOTING, BECAUSE THE MOTHERING PLATFORM I INHERITED FROM SOCIETY HAS PROVEN ITSELF SLIPPERY.

I STAND WITH THE IDEA THAT MOTHERHOOD IS NOT A MONOCROP. WE'RE NOT MEANT TO GROW IN ISOLATION. WHEN WE COME TOGETHER AND TAKE UP SPACE, RELEASING FEAR, GUILT, AND SHAME, THE LOVE-WATTAGE OF CONNECTION ALONE CAN REBOOT OUR SYSTEMS AND SHIFT US TOWARD HOME.

MAY THESE 40 QUIPS AND QUESTIONS INCREASE YOUR SURFACE AREA AND SHARPEN YOUR SENSES, DEEPENING DIRECT CONTACT WITH LIFE (WHILE CAPTURING A SACRED SLICE OF HERSTORY).

THANKFULLY,

GINA TANG
CREATIVE DIRECTOR
THE REGENERATIVE WRITING INSTITUTE

SUGGESTED USE:

– EXPRESS DAILY.

– ANSWER QUESTIONS IN ANY ORDER
& AT ANY PACE.

– WORK WITH A PARTNER OR SMALL GROUP.

– DROP ALL JUDGMENTS, FILTERS & CENSORS.

– GO HANDS-FREE
USING VOICE MEMO, TEXT, OR VIDEO.

– MAKE IT A MEMOIR:
WRITE FREELY IN A SPIRAL NOTEBOOK FIRST,
THEN TRANSFER SELECTED ANSWERS
TO THE PAGES OF THIS JOURNAL.

FOR MORE TIPS, VISIT
MOTHERHOODEXPRESS.ORG

HERE YOU ARE.

WHERE IS IT, EXACTLY?

WHAT DO YOU NOTICE
ABOUT YOUR INNER AND OUTER ENVIRONMENTS?

DESCRIBE WHAT YOU SEE, HEAR, SMELL, FEEL,
AND SENSE.

ARE YOU IN PAST, OR PRESENT-TENSE?
WHAT'S HAPPENING IN YOUR SPACE?

NAVIGATION TAKES PATIENCE, AND GRACE.

QUESTION #1
WHERE ARE YOU NOW?

HELLO, SNOWFLAKE.

YOU ARE ONE-OF-A-KIND.

WHAT ILLUMINATES
YOUR UNIQUE
AND WILD
SHAPE?

QUESTION #2
WHEN DO YOU FEEL BEAUTIFUL?

ONCE UPON A TIME,
YOUR HEAD TOLD YOU A TALE.

AT THIS POINT,
IT MIGHT BE RUNNING ON RAILS.

LET'S TRACK IT.

QUESTION #3
WHAT'S YOUR STORY?

LAUGHTER IS THE FRUIT OF THE SOUL:
ALWAYS IN SEASON,
AND RIPE FOR THE PICKING.

EVEN WHEN IT'S NOT ORGANIC,
IT STILL BOOSTS YOUR IMMUNE SYSTEM,
AND LIGHTENS YOUR LOAD.

LET YOURSELF BE TICKLED
EASILY, AND OFTEN.

(SMILING HELPS SOFTEN
YOUR SIDES.)

QUESTION #4
WHAT'S SO FUNNY?

REGARDLESS OF WHERE, HOW, OR WHEN
YOU OCCUPY YOUR OCCUPATIONS,
AND REGARDLESS OF WHAT YOU DO,
THERE ARE JOB EXPECTATIONS,
AND PERFORMANCE REVIEWS.

HOW IS WORKING
WORKING FOR YOU?

QUESTION #5
WHO DO YOU WORK FOR?

SOMETIMES NEW SKIN FEELS LIKE OLD SHOES:
TOO TIGHT IN SOME PLACES,
IN OTHERS, TOO LOOSE.

WHERE MIGHT RESISTANCE, TENSION, TERROR,
FRUSTRATION, EXHAUSTION, IRRITATION,
OR OTHER CONSTRICTING SENSATIONS
BE SITTING
IN YOUR BODY?
IN YOUR MIND?

QUESTION #6
WHERE ARE YOU TIGHT?

THERE'S NO PLACE LIKE HOME,
AND NO TWO HOMES ALIKE.

WHO MODELED YOURS?
HOW HAS IT BEEN UPDATED?
WHAT IS IT FOUNDED UPON?

QUESTION #7
WHAT KIND OF HOUSE ARE YOU HOLDING?

PAR FOR THE COURSE
OF HUMAN NATURE,
YOU CARRY A SENSE OF SELF.

IT WAS HANDED DOWN TO YOU,
VERY EARLY ON.

RARELY ARE WE ADVISED,
UPON RECEIPT,
THAT WE'RE ABLE TO EXCHANGE IT.

QUESTION #8
WHO DO YOU THINK YOU ARE?

SMALL AS THEY ARE,
BABIES TAKE UP A LOT OF ROOM.
ADD THAT TO PRE-EXISTING CHILDREN,
PARTNERS, EXTENDED FAMILY MEMBERS,
EVERYBODY'S SCHEDULES.
ARE YOU KEEPING EVERY ONE/THING
ALIVE? IN LINE?

WHERE, IN THE MIDST OF IT ALL,
DO YOU HAVE TIME
FOR *YOU?*

WHERE IS THERE SPACE
INTO WHICH
NO ONE ELSE'S
SOCKS CAN FALL?

QUESTION #9
WHEN IS YOUR "ME" TIME?

BEARING WITNESS TO YOU ALONE,
WHAT'S YOUR GENERAL POSTURE?
WHAT'S YOUR OVERALL TONE?

MIND YOUR
MANNERS,
MEANS,
AND METHODS.

ARE YOU IN A HURRY?
ARE YOU GOING SLOW?
ARE YOU OPEN?
ARE YOU CLOSED?

THERE'S NOTHING RIGHT OR WRONG
BUT AWARENESS MAKES IT SO.

QUESTION #10
HOW ARE YOU *DOING?*

MOVING WITH THE CURRENT
MEANS LETTING GO OF THE CURB.

WHY DOES UNCERTAINTY MAKE US NERVOUS?

WHY CLING TO THE SHORES OF EXPERIENCE
WHEN ALL WE SEEK TO CONTROL MOVES, TOO?

SOMETIMES, DO YOU FIND
IT EASY TO RELEASE—
UNWIND—
AND LET THE DIVINE WASH THROUGH?

QUESTION #11
WHAT FLOWS?

YOU ARE AN INSTRUMENT
IN THE HAND OF A MASTER-
CRAFTER OF A CUSTOM REALITY.

ANYTHING CAN BE INCORPORATED
INTO YOUR BODY OF WORK.

THE BEST TOOLS GET SHARPER WITH USE.

QUESTION #12
WHERE DO YOU SHARPEN YOUR TOOLS?

EVERY LIVING PERSON
COMES EQUIPPED
WITH A BIOLOGICAL SAFETY MONITOR.

YOU ARE WIRED TO NOTICE
WHEN THE ICE GROWS THIN,
OR THORNS CROWD IN,
OR THE FLOOR TURNS TO EGGSHELLS,
OR NO ONE CAN HEAR YOU.

KNOWING YOUR NETWORK,
AND THAT YOUR NETS WORK,
KEEPS YOU IN THE GREEN.

QUESTION #13
WHO CAN YOU TRUST?

EAT REAL FOOD,
BE GENERALLY HEALTHY.

BUT WHOLE HEALTH
MEANS MORE
THAN WHOLE FOODS.

YOU HAVE OTHER SYSTEMS, TOO.

QUESTION #14
WHAT NOURISHES YOU?

THE EARTH IS MOSTLY WATER.
THE BODY IS MOSTLY WATER.

RAIN COMES:
ERODING OLD EDGES,
CLEARING AND CLEANSING,
NURTURING GROWTH.

THEN WHY ARE WE TOLD
TO HOLD BACK OUR TEARS?

DO NOT DOUBT
THE WISDOM IN THE TRICKLES,
OR THE FLOODS.

QUESTION #15
WHEN DO YOU CRY?

WHEN YOU RISE,
DO YOU SHINE?

OR DO YOU NEED TIME,
SPACE, AND DUE PROCESS
TO BOARD THE VESSEL
OF YOUR BODY
AND EMBARK INTO THE FRAY?
(THIS IS TOTALLY OKAY.)

THE WORLD
CHANGES
WHENEVER
YOU AWAKEN—
WITH EACH
AND EVERY
BLINK OF AN I.

QUESTION #16
HOW DO YOU FEEL WHEN YOU WAKE UP?

ACTUALLY, THE ANSWER TO
THIS QUESTION IS UNCONDITIONAL:
YES.

WE ONLY FORGET
BECAUSE LIGHT CASTS SHADOW.

WE ONLY FORGET
SO WE CAN REMEMBER.

WE ONLY FALL OUT
SO WE CAN FALL BACK IN.

QUESTION #17
ARE YOU IN LOVE?

YOU ARE LITERALLY MADE OF STARS.
FIRE & COMBUSTION
ARE PART OF THE PACKAGE.

AN ANGRY WOMAN IS A FORCE
OF NATURE.

(IT'S NO WONDER THE PATRIARCHAL
CONSUMER CAPITALIST COMPLEX
WOULD TRY TO TAMP HER DOWN.)

WHAT YOU FEEL CAN BE HEALED.

WHAT YOU DON'T ALLOW
YOURSELF TO FEEL
BECOMES A BLACK AND HUNGRY HOLE.

QUESTION #18
WHAT ANGERS YOU?

ACCORDING TO PHYSICAL LAW,
EVERY ACTION
HAS AN EQUAL AND OPPOSITE
REACTION.

THERE ARE SO MANY FACTIONS
PULLING US UP AND OUT OF OURSELVES,
PUSHING US SIDEWAYS, SCATTERED, OR SCARCE.

WHAT HOLDS YOU DOWN?
HOW DO YOU GROUND?

QUESTION #19
WHAT ANCHORS YOU?

WHEN YOU HAVE A BABY,
YOU MAY BE
TOO TIRED
TO DO ANYTHING
EXTRA.

WITHOUT CASTING ANYTHING NEW,
WHAT ARE YOU ALREADY DOING—
EATING, GROOMING, ROCKING,
SINGING, WALKING, TALKING—
THAT COULD STAND A RE-STRUCTURE?

WORK YOUR MAGIC.
YOUR MAGIC WORKS.

QUESTION #20
WHAT ROUTINES CAN BE MADE RITUAL?

CONSIDER AN INVENTORY:

WHAT BELIEFS, ATTACHMENTS,
EXPECTATIONS, OPINIONS,
JUDGMENTS, HABITS,
BURDENS, BAGGAGE,
OR OTHER WEIGHTS

MIGHT BE TAKING
YOU AWAY
FROM WHAT
YOU WANT?

QUESTION #21
WHAT HAVE YOU GOT TO LOSE?

"STICKS AND STONES
MAY BREAK MY BONES
BUT WORDS WILL NEVER HURT ME."

THIS IS PROVEN FALSE.

WHAT WE SAY TO OURSELVES
AND EACH OTHER
SHAPES EVERY EDGE
OF REALITY.

SPEAK,
FOR HUMAN-SAKE.

QUESTION #22
HOW DO YOU USE YOUR WORDS?

HELP =

HAVING
EFFECTIVE
LIFE
PROPS

(DON'T MAKE HOME WITHOUT THEM.)

QUESTION #23
WHO CAN YOU ASK FOR HELP?

UPON CLOSER INSPECTION,
THE HEART IS MUCH MORE
THAN A PUMP.

IT HAS POWERS OF PERCEPTION,
AND ITS OWN PIECE OF MIND.

QUESTION #24
WHAT IS YOUR HEART'S DESIRE?

IN THE SHALLOWS,
YOU SURVIVE.

IN THE DEPTHS,
YOU THRIVE.

QUESTION #25
HOW IS YOUR BREATHING?

LET FOOD BE YOUR MEDICINE,
AND MEDICINE YOUR FOOD.
IF YOU ARE WHAT YOU EAT,
THEN REAL FOOD HEALS YOU.

PROCESSED FOODS
REQUIRE PROCESSING TOO—
SQUANDERING FUEL.

THEN THERE ARE TIMES
WHEN FAMINE IS A FEELING.
WHEN SOMETHING ELSE
IS EATING YOU—
SO YOU TAKE THE FIRST BITE
LIKE YOU MIGHT GET
A HEAD OF IT.

QUESTION #26
WHAT ARE YOU EATING?

INNER COMPASS,
SET THE COURSE.

THE BODY KNOWS THE WAY.

LISTENING IN,
FEELING OUT.

TAKING YOUR TIME
IS ALL THAT COUNTS.

ALLOWING THE PATH
TO UNFOLD
AT YOUR FEET—
YOU ARE WORTH EVERY STEP,
AND THE PAUSES BETWEEN.

QUESTION #27
WHAT'S YOUR NEXT MOVE?

PROBING
POTENCY

INVESTIGATING
INITIATIVE

EXPLORING
ENTHUSIASM

DISCOVERING
DRIVE

QUESTION #28
WHAT'S ALIVE IN YOU?

YOUR CENTRAL PROCESSING UNIT
IS HIGHLY INTELLIGENT.

LIKE ANY OPERATING SYSTEM,
IT RECEIVES DOWNLOADS
FROM CULTURE, ANCESTRY,
AND OTHER SOURCES.

LIKE ANY OPERATING SYSTEM,
IT NEEDS THE OCCASIONAL
DEFRAGMENTING, REBOOTING,
RESTORING, AND LIVE UPDATE.

OPEN YOUR TASK MANAGER.
CHECK YOUR ENERGY USAGE.
ANYTHING PHISHY?

QUESTION #29
WHAT PROGRAMS ARE YOU RUNNING?

BIOMES HAVE BALANCE,
AND A NEED FOR CONTAINER.

FILTERING THE ELEMENTS—
INTERCONNECTED,
YET INDIVIDUAL.

YOUR MEMBRANES
ARE SEMI-PERMEABLE
ON PURPOSE.

PROTECTION
IS A FORM OF LOVE.

QUESTION #30
WHERE ARE YOUR BOUNDARIES?

IT'S NOT THE SIZE
OF THE QUESTION
THAT COUNTS.

EVERY LIFE,
AND EVERY DAY,
HAS DOUBTS.

BUT EVERY LIFE,
AND EVERY DAY,
HAS A RIGHT
TO COME
AS IT MAY.

QUESTION #31
WHAT ARE YOU HERE FOR?

THE ABILITY TO BRING LIFE
INTO THE WORLD
IS A POWER ABOVE MOST OTHERS.

AND, YOU ARE EXTRAORDINARY
IN OTHER WAYS, TOO.

ACCOUNT FOR THE HEROICS OF YOU—
THE THINGS YOU DO
EFFORTLESSLY,
INNATELY,
TO BRING MORE LIFE
TO THE LIFE YOU BRING.

QUESTION #32
WHAT ARE YOUR SUPER POWERS?

LOOK BENEATH YOU.

LOOK BEHIND YOU.

LOOK INSIDE YOU.

WHAT TETHERS YOU
TO THIS PARTICULAR
TIME-SPACE EXTENSION?

QUESTION #33
WHERE ARE YOUR ROOTS?

GRATITUDE
IS A GATEWAY:

TO PEACE
TO PROSPERITY
TO PATIENCE
TO POWER
TO PERSEVERANCE
TO PARTNERSHIP
TO PRESENCE
TO POLLINATION
TO PRAYER

QUESTION #34
WHAT ARE YOU THANKFUL FOR?

WHAT YOU GET
IS WHAT YOU SEE.

(OBJECTIVES IN THE MIRROR
ARE CLOSER THAN THEY APPEAR.)

QUESTION #35
WHERE ARE YOUR BLIND SPOTS?

THINK OF
THE PEOPLE
WHO PROVE
THAT WHAT YOU
DREAM
IS POSSIBLE.

QUESTION #36
WHO INSPIRES YOU?

SOMETIMES WE MAKE SOMETHING
STRONGER BY HIDING FROM IT.

THROW BACK THE CURTAINS.
LIFT THE VEILS.
OPEN THE CLOSET.
SHOW YOUR FACE.

COURAGE NEEDS A SHARPENING EDGE.

WHAT HOLDS YOU CAPTIVE
SETS YOU FREE.

QUESTION #37
WHAT DO YOU FEAR?

WHILE HISTORY
MAY INDEED
REPEAT ITSELF,

THE HISTORY
THAT MATTERS MOST
IS THE ONE
IN THE MAKING.

QUESTION #38
WHAT IS TRUE TODAY?

WITH NEW SEASONS
COME DIFFERENT SEEDS.

EVERY CONNECTION
GROWS ITS OWN TREE.

QUESTION #39
HOW DO YOU PICK YOUR PEOPLE?

FOLLOW YOUR BLISS,
SAYS JOSEPH CAMPBELL,
AND THE UNIVERSE WILL OPEN DOORS
WHERE BEFORE
THERE WERE WALLS.

GREAT NEWS, INDEED!

THIS MEANS
WHATEVER MAKES YOU HAPPY
OFFERS YOU HOPE.

QUESTION #40
WHAT BRINGS YOU JOY?

...AND THAT'S ALL SHE WROTE,
FOR TODAY.

THE KEY IS THAT SHE WROTE,
TODAY.

EVERY TIME SHE SHOWS UP
AND MAKES SPACE
FOR HER VOICE—

EVERY TIME SHE LISTENS
TO WHAT SHE HEARS
AND HONORS HER TRUTH—

EVERY TIME SHE IS SEEN
IN WHO, AND HOW, SHE IS—

SOMETHING ESSENTIAL TAKES PLACE.

AND EVERY INSTANCE
OF THAT WHICH IS ESSENTIAL
MAKES THE WORLD SAFER,
AND MORE SOUND.

THANK YOU FOR CHOOSING
MOTHERHOOD EXPRESS.

FOR EVERY JOURNAL PURCHASED,
ANOTHER IS GIFTED.

LEARN MORE, EXPLORE WORKSHOPS,
BUY JOURNALS, AND MAKE TAX-DEDUCTIBLE
DONATIONS AT MOTHERHOODEXPRESS.ORG

FOR OTHER USEFUL PUBLICATIONS
@ THE REGENERATIVE WRITING INSTITUTE
VISIT REGENERATIVEWRITINGINSTITUTE.COM

www.ingramcontent.com/pod-product-compliance
Lightning Source LLC
Chambersburg PA
CBHW052103110526
44591CB00013B/2329